YEMENI ABC

Discover Yemeni culture one letter at a time!

Esmihan Almontaser

To Yemeni children around the world, may you carry your culture in your heart, stand proud in your heritage and share the beauty of your traditions with the world and the generations to come

Text copyright © 2025 by Esmihan Almontaser
Illustrations copyright © 2025 by Wara Warart

ISBN 979-8-9991607-0-6

Special thanks to Vimto for granting permission to use an image of their product in this book.

This Book Belongs to:

_____

Aa

Aseed

Bb

Bakhoor

Cc

Camel

Dd

Dar al-Hajar

E e

Eid

F f

Farshah

Gg

Gishr

Hh

Haneeth

Ii

Island of Socotra

Jj

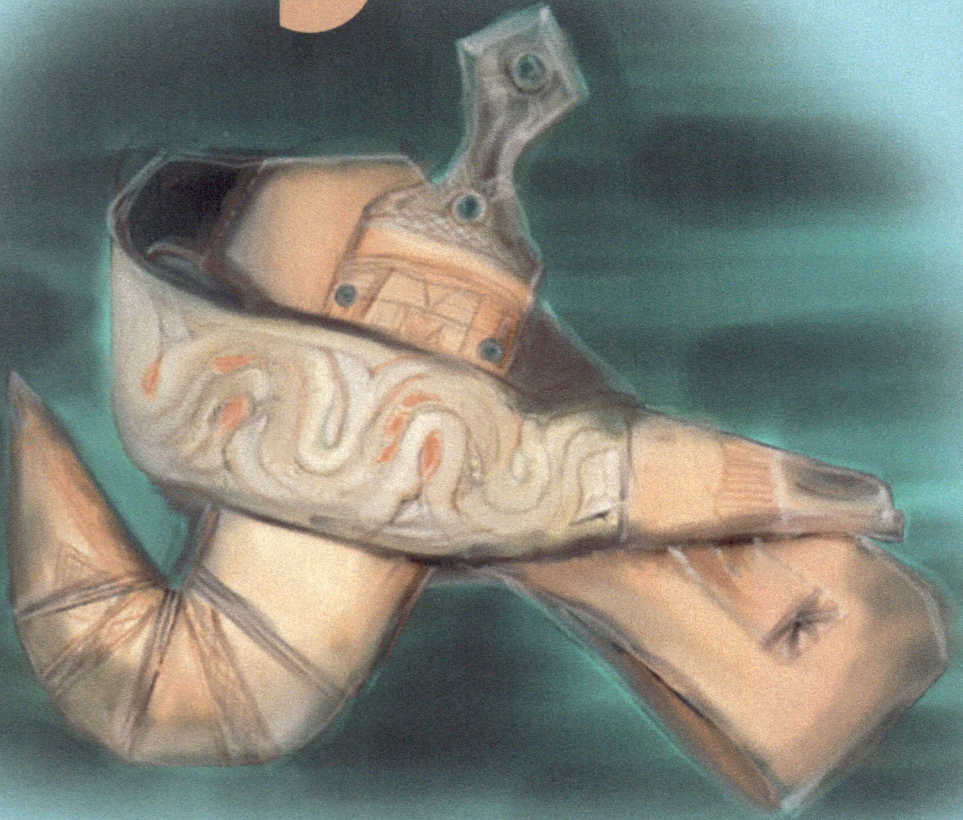

Jambiyah

Kk

Khaliat al-Nahl

L l

Lahooh

Mm

Maswan

Nn

Neighborhood
of Shibam

Old City of Sanaa

P p

Port of Aden

Qq

Qamariah

R r

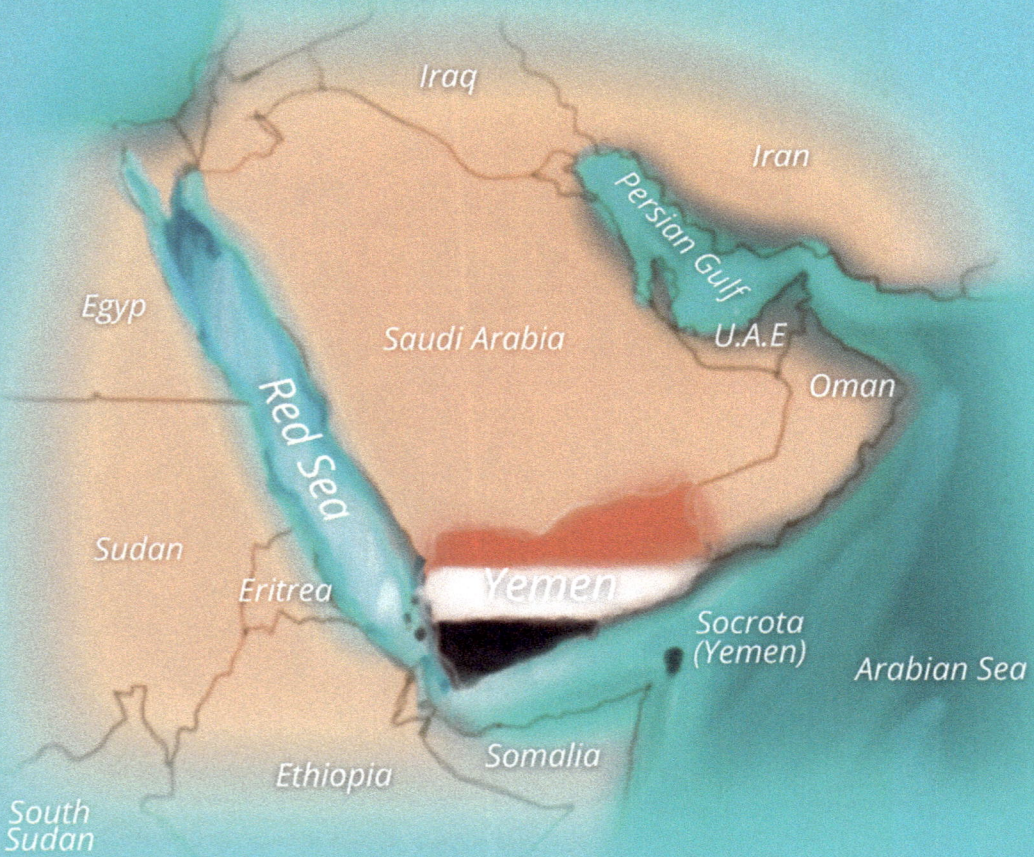

Iraq

Iran

Persian Gulf

Egyp

Saudi Arabia

U.A.E

Oman

Red Sea

Sudan

Eritrea

Yemen

Socrota
(Yemen)

Arabian Sea

Somalia

South
Sudan

Ethiopia

Red Sea

S s

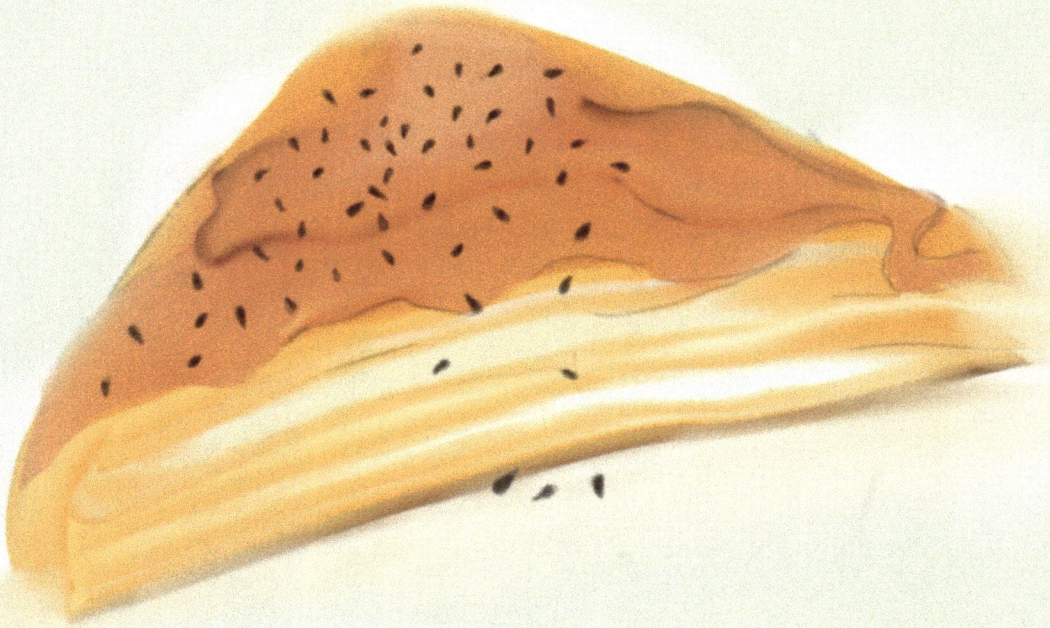

Sabaya

Tt

Taiz

U u

Ummi

V v

Vimto

Ww

Wadi

Xx

Extra Resilient

Y y

Yemenis

Z z

Zebeeb

Glossary

Aseed

Aseed is a traditional Yemeni dish made from flour and water, churned with a long wooden tool called a mihwash until smooth and soft. It's shaped like a dome, with a dip in the center filled with flavorful meat stew, making it look like a volcano! Aseed is eaten using the right hand, scooping it up with two fingers. The stew often includes condiments like hilba (whipped fenugreek) and sahawig (a spicy blend of tomatoes, jalapeños, garlic and cilantro).

Bakhoor

Bakhoor is a fragrant incense that is burned over charcoal in a decorative burner called a mabkhara. The aromatic smoke fills the house with a beautiful scent, especially during Eid or when guests arrive. Yemeni women also use bakhoor to scent their hair and clothes.

Camel

The camel is a desert animal known for its humped back and ability to travel long distances without water. While cars are common in Yemen today, camels are still used in some areas to carry cargo. It is not unusual to spot one walking down the road!

Dar al-Hajar

Meaning "Stone House" in Arabic, Dar al-Hajar is a stunning structure built into a rock in the capital city of Sana'a. It was used as a home for royalty and is now a museum that shows off Yemen's incredible architecture and history.

Eid

Yemenis celebrate two major Islamic holidays: Eid al-Fitr, which marks the end of Ramadan and Eid al-Adha, celebrated about two months later. These joyful occasions include special prayers, family gatherings, giving charity to those in need, gifts and delicious food.

Farshah

Farshah refers to Yemeni floor seating like cushions, mats, and ottomans arranged along the walls of a room. These comfy, low to the ground setups are often decorated in colorful, traditional patterns and are perfect for lounging, meals and gatherings.

Gishr

Gishr is a hot drink made by brewing dried coffee cherry husks with spices like ginger, cinnamon and caraway seeds. It's lightly sweetened and like tea, offers a comforting and aromatic alternative to coffee.

Haneeth

Haneeth is a flavorful Yemeni dish of slow-roasted lamb or chicken served over spiced rice. It's seasoned with a special blend called hawayij, a mix of black pepper, cumin, coriander, turmeric and cardamom and often prepared for feasts and celebrations.

Island of Socotra

Socotra is an island off the coast of Yemen, known for its unique plants and animals that aren't found anywhere else. One of its most famous features is the Dragon Blood Tree, with its umbrella shape and red sap used for medicinal purposes. The island is on the UNESCO World Heritage Site list.

Jambiyah

A jambiyah is a curved dagger worn at the waist by Yemeni men and boys, especially during special occasions. The handle of a Yemeni jambiyah reflects a person's wealth and social status. It's a symbol of tradition, pride and cultural identity.

Khaliat al-Nahl

Khaliat al-Nahl is called "Honeycomb Bread." This soft, fluffy pastry is shaped like a beehive and filled with sweet cream cheese. It's baked until golden, sprinkled with black nigella seeds and drizzled with honey. It's a popular breakfast treat, especially with tea.

Lahooh

Lahooh is a soft, spongy, pancake-like bread made from a fermented batter of flour, water and yeast. It's served with savory stews and is perfect for scooping food with your hands.

Maswan

Maswan is a traditional fabric with bold vertical stripes in red, black, yellow and silver. It's a unique part of Yemeni fashion and is worn proudly during weddings, celebrations and cultural events.

Neighborhood of Shibam

Shibam is a historic city famous for its towering mudbrick buildings, earning it the nickname "Manhattan of the Desert." Built in the 16th century and surrounded by protective walls, it's one of Yemen's UNESCO World Heritage Sites.

Old City of Sana'a

Sana'a, Yemen's capital, is one of the world's oldest continuously inhabited cities. Its Old City features tall buildings decorated with white pattern qamariahs, narrow alleyways and vibrant markets. It's a UNESCO World Heritage Site.

Port of Aden

Located by the Red Sea and the Gulf of Aden, this ancient port city has long been a hub for international trade. Ships from around the world have docked here for centuries to exchange goods and cultures.

Qamariah

Qamariahs are half-moon shaped window decorations made of multicolored stained glass. These beautiful features let in light while adding charm and color to traditional Yemeni homes. The name means "moonlike."

Red Sea

The Red Sea lies between the Arabian Peninsula and Northeast Africa. It's an important waterway for trade and travel and it's how Yemeni merchants connected with the world for centuries.

Sabaya

Sabaya, also known as Bint al-Sahn, is a flaky pastry made with layers of dough, butter and black seeds. It is often topped with sidr honey, one of the finest honeys in the world. It's a celebratory dish served to guests or on special occasions.

Taiz

Taiz is an ancient hilly city in southwestern Yemen known for its breathtaking views and coffee farms. It's the third largest city in Yemen and a center of culture, history and learning.

Ummi

Ummi means "my mother" in Arabic. Mothers hold a deeply respected role in Yemeni families. They are caretakers, teachers and keepers of tradition. In the Arab world, Mother's Day is celebrated on March 21.

Vimto

Vimto is a sweet fruit-flavored syrup that's mixed with water and served cold. It's especially popular during Ramadan and nearly every Yemeni household has a bottle ready for iftar (the fast-breaking meal).

Wadi

A wadi is a valley that becomes lush and green when it rains. These riverbeds run between mountains and are often used for farming when the water flows. There are many towns near wadis.

Extra Resilient

Yemenis are known for their strength and perseverance. No matter what challenges they face, they continue to work hard, stay hopeful and take care of one another.

Yemenis

People from Yemen are called Yemenis. Family is at the heart of Yemeni life and elders are treated with great respect. Generosity, hospitality and community are core values.

Zebeeb

Zebeeb are sweet, dried raisins, often white or purple, served alongside nuts like pistachios and cashews when guests visit. It's a warm and welcoming tradition.

www.ingramcontent.com/pod-product-compliance
Lightning Source LLC
Chambersburg PA
CBHW040835300326
41914CB00060B/1358